ALLIGATORS AND CROCODILES CAN'T CHEW!

AND OTHER AMAZING FACTS

By Thea Feldman
Illustrated by Lee Cosgrove

Ready-to-Read

An imprint of Simon & Schuster Children's Publishing Division
New York London Toronto Sydney New Delhi
1230 Avenue of the Americas, New York, New York 10020
This Simon Spotlight edition January 2021

For information about special discounts for bulk purchases, please contact Simon & Schuster Special Sales at 1-866-506-1949
or business@simonandschuster.com.
Manufactured in the United States of America 1020 LAK
2 4 6 8 10 9 7 5 3 1
Library of Congress Cataloging-in-Publication Data
Names: Feldman, Thea, author. | Cosgrove, Lee, illustrator. Title: Alligators and crocodiles can't chew! : and other amazing facts / by Thea
Feldman ; illustrated by Lee Cosgrove. Description: New York : Simon Spotlight, 2021. | Series: Super facts for super kids | Summary: "A nonfiction
Level 2 Ready-to-Read filled with fun facts about what makes alligators and crocodiles super"—Provided by publisher.
Identifiers: LCCN 2020020159 (print) | LCCN 2020020160 (eBook) | ISBN 9781534479791 (paperback) | ISBN 9781534479807 (hardcover) |
ISBN 9781534479814 (eBook) Subjects: LCSH: Alligators—Juvenile literature. | Crocodiles—Juvenile literature.
Classification: LCC QL666.C925 F47 2020 (print) | LCC QL666.C925 (eBook) | DDC 597.98/4—dc23
LC record available at https://lccn.loc.gov/2020020159 | LC eBook record available at https://lccn.loc.gov/2020020160

GLOSSARY

apex predator: an animal that is not eaten or hunted by other animals in the wild

brackish water: water that is saltier than fresh water but not as salty as salt water

caiman: a crocodilian that is very closely related to alligators

cold-blooded: having a body temperature that matches the temperature of its surroundings

crocodilians: a group of animal species including crocodiles, alligators, caimans, and gharials; all crocodilians have powerful bites, many teeth, short legs, webbed back feet, long tails, and thick bony-plated skin

endangered: at risk of disappearing forever

gharial: a crocodilian with a long, thin snout

keystone species: an animal or plant that helps other animals and plants survive in the same area

prey: an animal hunted by a predator

reptile: a cold-blooded animal whose body is usually covered in scales or bony plates

wetland: a place where the ground is soft, wet, and often flooded; swamps and marshes are different kinds of wetlands

Note to readers: Some of these words may have more than one definition. The definitions above match how these words are used in this book.

CONTENTS

Did you know that alligators and crocodiles have some of the strongest bites in the world? They might have an impressive bite, but they actually can't chew!

By the time you finish this book, you'll know a lot of amazing facts about alligators and crocodiles!

CHAPTER 1

IS IT AN ALLIGATOR OR A CROCODILE?

Both alligators and crocodiles are crocodilians (say: krah-kuh-DIH-lee-uhns).

alligators

caimans (say: KAY-muhns) are crocodilians that are very similar to alligators.

Crocodilians are a group of animals with long tails, short legs, webbed back feet, many pointed teeth, and thick bony-plated skin.

crocodilians

gharials
(say: GAIR-ee-uhls)
have long, thin snouts.

crocodiles

How can you tell an alligator from a crocodile?

One way is to look at the snout!

Alligator: Rounded and U-shaped

Crocodile: Pointed and V-shaped

Alligators have rounded snouts and crocodiles have pointed snouts.

If you see only

the animal's top teeth

when the mouth is closed,

the animal is an alligator.

If you see top and bottom teeth

when the mouth is closed,

it's a crocodile.

Alligators live in wetlands
with soft and wet ground,
near freshwater lakes and rivers.

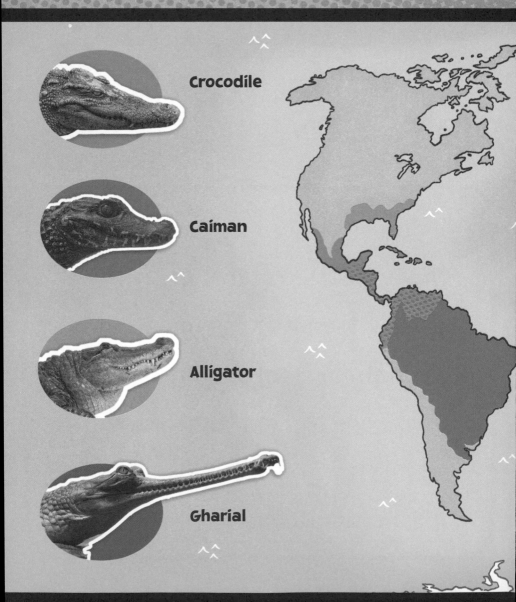

Crocodile

Caiman

Alligator

Gharial

Most crocodiles live in salt water or brackish (say: BRAK-ish) water, which is saltier than fresh water but not as salty as salt water.

South Florida is the only place in the wild where alligators and crocodiles both live.

Most crocodiles are also larger than alligators.

Cuvier's dwarf caiman: about 5 feet

American alligator: about 11 feet

four standard shopping carts: about 12 feet

American crocodile: about 15 feet

saltwater crocodile: up to 23 feet

One thing that crocodiles
and alligators do have in common
is that they can climb trees!
Scientists think they climb
to warm up their bodies
and to check out their surroundings.
Now you can be an expert at
spotting alligators and crocodiles!

CHAPTER 2
IN AND OUT OF THE WATER

Crocodilians spend

most of their time in the water,

but they feel at home

both underwater and on land.

Their eyes, ears, and nostrils stay above the water's surface while the rest of their body is underwater.

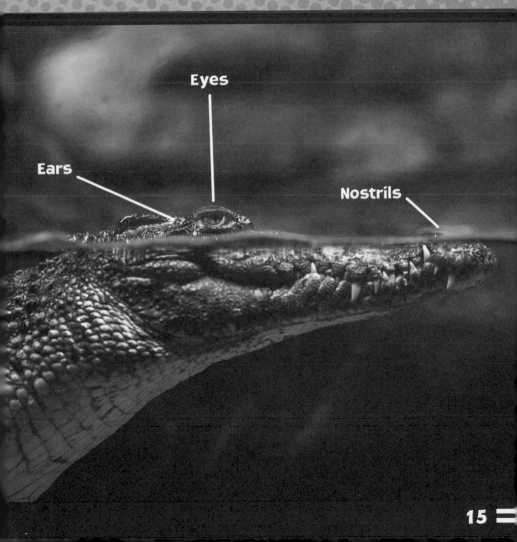

Eyes

Ears

Nostrils

When it's time to dive, crocodilians have things covered . . . literally!

Special eyelids protect their eyes so that they can see underwater.

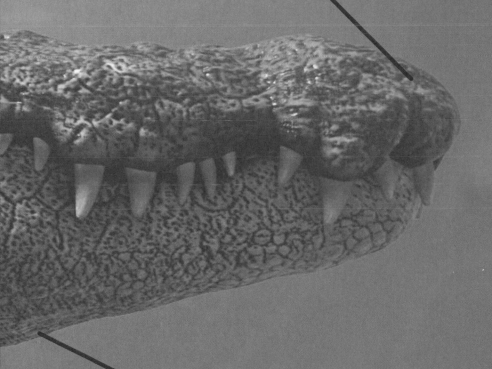

Crocodilians can stay underwater for 2 hours!

Ears and nostrils close tight to keep water from entering.

A special flap at the back of the throat keeps water out.

When a crocodilian crawls onto land, its webbed feet help it move through muddy, shallow water. Then it lies in the sun to warm up.

Crocodilians are cold-blooded reptiles. This means their body temperatures match the temperature outside.

If they get hot, crocodilians open their mouths to cool off. Reptiles can't sweat!

Female crocodilians go on land to lay eggs. They may lay as many as 90 eggs at once!

The temperature of the nest decides if the babies are female or male.

91.4 degrees Fahrenheit and above: Most American alligator babies are male.

86 degrees Fahrenheit and below: Most American alligator babies are female.

Once the babies hatch,
the mother gently scoops
up to 15 newborns at a time
into her mouth and carries them
to the water.

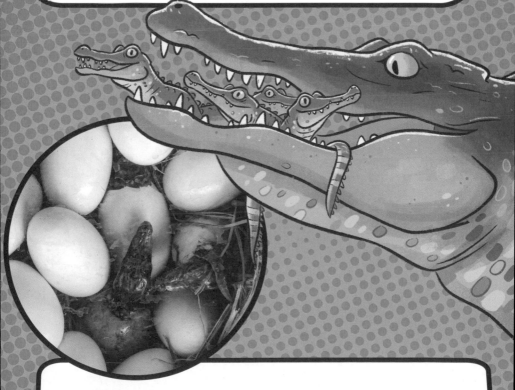

The babies will grow up both
in water and on land.

Crocodilians can slam their jaws shut 6 times faster than you can blink. Their bite forces are some of the strongest in the world.

Some Bite Strengths to Chew On...

HUMAN
ABOUT 160 PSI
(POUNDS PER SQUARE INCH)

LION
ABOUT 1,000 PSI

However, crocodilians can't chew! They don't have the muscles to move their jaws like that.

Pounds per square inch (psi) is a unit used to measure the amount of pressure placed on something.

SALTWATER CROCODILE ABOUT 3,700 PSI

If crocodilians can't chew,

how do they eat?

They swallow small animals whole

and use their sharp teeth

to break apart larger ones.

They also swallow stones, which stay in their stomachs and help grind up food.

Crocodilians digest their food slowly. Some can go without eating for a year!

Crocodilians are fierce animals that hunt and eat other animals called prey (say: PRAY).
They eat all kinds of prey, including fish, frogs, birds, deer, and even other crocodilians!

Some crocodilians are

apex predators

(say: AY-pecks PRED-uh-turs).

This means that

they aren't hunted or eaten

by other animals in the wild.

While American alligators are hungry predators, they also help other animals. They dig big holes in the ground to create small ponds. When the dry season comes, the alligator holes are rare sources of water until the wet season starts again.

Other animals use the holes
for water too. The alligator eats
some of these animals,
but most are able to stay alive.
Because other animals depend
on the American alligator to survive,
it is called a keystone species
(say: KEE-stoen SPEE-sheez).

If you could be like a crocodilian, what would you want to do? Would you want to grow a long tail, stay underwater for 2 hours, or quickly snap your jaws shut?

Whatever you decide, one thing is for certain: alligators and crocodiles are amazing!

Turn the page to learn about protecting alligators and crocodiles!

Many crocodilians are endangered, which means they are at risk of disappearing forever. This is because people hunt them for food and for their skin. People are also destroying and moving into the areas where crocodilians live.

In the 1960s, the American alligator population was quickly disappearing. The American government passed laws that made it illegal to hunt alligators. They also protected alligator land and started a breeding program. Thanks to these efforts, the American alligator is no longer endangered. This success story provides hope for other endangered crocodilians.

How can you help alligators and crocodiles? Tell your family and friends not to buy clothes and other items made from animal skin. If you live near a wetland, you can volunteer to help clean up garbage that can hurt the animals living there. Your actions can help a super crocodilian!